KNOW THE GAME

Swimming

D0433258

Produced in
collaboration with the
Amateur Swimming
Association

Second edition

Swimming

Produced in collaboration with the Amateur Swimming Association

Published by A & C Black (Publishers) Ltd
35 Bedford Row, London WC1R 4JH

Second edition 2000

Copyright © 2000
Amateur Swimming Association

ISBN 0 7136 5264 0

A CIP catalogue record for this book is available from the British Library.

KNOW THE GAME is a registered trademark

Printed in Hong Kong

Contents

Acknowledgements
Thanks to Michael McKeever and the
English Volleyball Association, 27 South
Road, West Bridgford, Nottingham, NG2
7AG.
The publishers would like to thank the
International Volleyball Federation for
their contribution to this book.
All action photography courtesy of
BM Totterdell.

Note Throughout the book players and
officials are referred to individually as
'he'. This should, of course, be taken to
mean 'he or she' where appropriate.

Foreword

Several hundred thousand copies of *Know The Game Volleyball* have been sold since I wrote the first edition in 1958. For over 40 years now the policy, which I established, has been that all royalties go to the national volleyball association to further promote the game; I am glad that this will continue into the new millennium.

When volleyball was first created in 1895, it was known as 'mintonette'; in Arab countries to this day it is called 'the flying ball'. I think this is a delightful image for our game, that is now, with football and basketball, one of the world's top three recreational games. However, volleyball is also an Olympic sport, an indoor game, a beach game and a park game. For old and young, girls and boys, able-bodied and disabled, the skills and movements of the game make it a complete and inexpensive physical education.

This edition has been revised by Michael McKeever, for many years the Technical Director of the English Volleyball Association. Knowing his understanding and passion for the game, and his grasp of the changes which creative games have to undergo, I can think of no one better qualified to help volleyball fly into the next century.

Don Anthony
Honorary President
English Volleyball Association

3

Introduction

The beginning

In 1895 William Morgan, the Physical Education Director at Holyoake YMCA gymnasium, invented a game in which an inflated bladder was 'batted' by two teams over a rope. Morgan wanted a simple sport which would be suitable for a variety of physical types, both fit and unfit, and which could be played almost anywhere. This game served the purpose, and was dubbed 'volleyball'.

A world sport

The game spread rapidly throughout the world and in 1947 the International Volleyball Federation (FIVB) was formed. In 1948 the first European Volleyball Championships were held, and in Tokyo in 1964 it became the first Olympic team sport for both men and women. In 1996 beach volleyball made its debut at the Olympic Games in Atlanta, and both sitting volleyball and standing volleyball for people with disabilities have been part of the Paralympic Games since 1976.

World Championships at Senior, Junior and Youth levels for men and women take place every four years. The World League (men) and the World Grand Prix (women) are played annually by the world's top 12 national teams for a prize fund of over $12 million. The five Continental Confederations hold their own championships every two years.

The World Beach Grand Prix and World Beach Volleyball Championships are also part of the never-ending calendar of major volleyball events, which stretches to all four corners of the globe.

Volleyball is now one of the most popular team games in the world with an estimated one billion players worldwide.

Characteristics of the game

Volleyball is a sport played by two teams on a court divided by a net. There are different versions of the game available for specific circumstances, e.g. mini volleyball (3 v 3) for children, 2 v 2 beach volleyball, recreational 4 v 4 park volleyball and sitting volleyball (for players with disabilities).

The object of the game is to send the ball over the net in order to ground it in the opponent's court, and to prevent the opponent doing the same. Each team is allowed three contacts to return the ball (in addition to the block contact).

The ball is put into play with a service from behind the baseline that sends the ball over the net and into the opponent's court. The rally continues until the ball is grounded on the playing court, goes 'out' or a team fails to return it properly.

In volleyball the team winning a rally scores a point (rally point system). When the receiving team wins a rally it scores a point and the right to serve. Its players rotate one position clockwise.

In beach volleyball only the serving team can win a point. If the receiving team wins the rally, it wins the right to serve, but does not win a point.

Facilities and equipment

The court

The playing area is 18 m long by 9 m wide, surrounded by a 'free zone' of at least 3 m.

Indoors, the playing surface should be flat, non-slip, non-abrasive, dry and clean. Ideally it should be shock absorbing, in order to reduce injuries that can be caused by repeated jumping and landing on a non-yielding surface. Volleyball can also be played outdoors on sand, or grass, which should be checked carefully for any sharp or dangerous objects.

▼ *Fig. 1 The court*

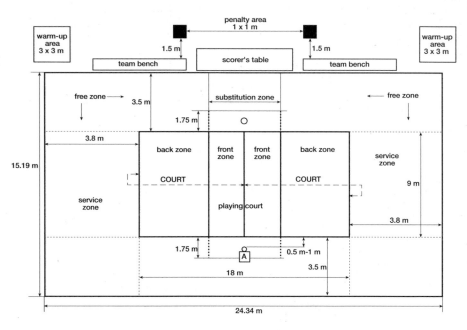

The net

The net is 2.43 m high for men and 2.24 m high for women. It is l m deep and 9.5 m long. It is essential that the net is taut, so that the ball will rebound from it.

Two flexible antennae are fastened to the net above the sidelines. The ball has to cross the net between the antennae.

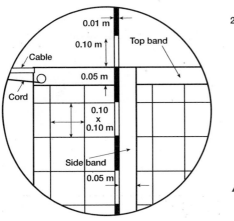

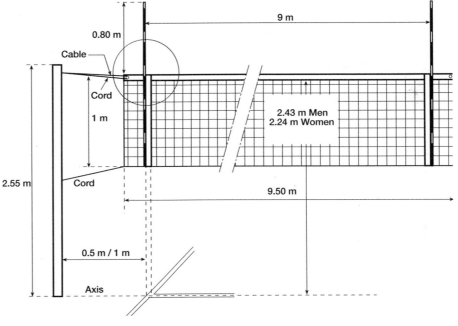

▲ *Fig. 2 Design of the net*

Posts

The posts must be rounded and smooth and be screwed to, or slotted into, the floor. They should have no dangerous or obstructing devices protruding from them. Free-standing or posts with weights are not permitted. Tie wires below head height should not be used to secure the posts. The posts must be between 0.5 m and 1 m from the court.

Referee stand

The referee sits or stands on a stand that is situated at one end of the net. His or her view must be approximately 0.5 m above the height of the net. The referee stand should present minimal obstruction to the players.

The ball

The ball is spherical, with a circumference of 65–67 cm and a weight of 260–280 g. It is made with a flexible leather or synthetic leather case, inside of which is a rubber bladder.

When first starting to play volleyball, the choice of ball is important. There are a number of excellent purpose-made teaching balls that are ideal for children. These approved balls are lighter than their match counterparts, and are widely available from educational suppliers.

Moulded rubber volleyballs sting the hands and bruise the arms and discourage beginners. These balls are not approved by the English Volleyball Association and should not be used.

Clothing

Team members wear uniform, numbered, numbered shirts, shorts, and sports shoes. Shirts are numbered from 1 through to 18 only, and the numbers are 20 cm high on the back, and 15 cm high on the front.

Players are forbidden from wearing any object that may cause injury, or give them an artificial advantage.

Some players wear protective kneepads to help them slide on the floor when attempting to retrieve a low ball.

Start of play

The teams

Each team consists of six players on court and a maximum of six substitutes (12 in total). If a team is reduced to less than six players, for example due to an injury or a sending-off, that team forfeits the match.

Choice of court

The two captains toss a coin and the winner either chooses to serve first or selects the court in which to start the match.

After each set, the teams change courts and the team that received service serves first in the following set.

Before the beginning of the decisive set, a coin is tossed once more to decide the choice of court or service.

In the last set, when one team has a total of eight points, the teams change courts; the team serving at the time of the change continues to serve.

Position of players prior to start of play

At the moment the ball is hit by the server all the other players must be standing on the court and in their correct positions. The three players who can play at the net (smash and block) are called *front row players* and occupy positions 4 (front left), 3 (front centre) and 2 (front right). The other three are *back row players* and occupy positions 5 (back left), 6 (back centre) and 1 (back right) (*see* fig. 3).

At the moment the ball is served each front row player must be nearer to the net than their corresponding back row player, i.e. the player in position 4 must be in front of the player in position 5, 3 in front of 6 and 2 in front of 1. Also, each side player must be closer to their corresponding side line than the middle player, i.e. 4 must be to the left of 3, 2 must be to the right of 3; and in the back row 5 must be to the left of 6 and 1 must be to the right of 6.

It is a fault if players are in the wrong rotational positions when the ball is served (*see* 'Rotation', page 11). The only exception to this rule occurs during service, when the server (player in position 1) may move anywhere along the baseline to serve.

Once the ball has been served the players may move around and occupy any position on their court. However back row players are not allowed to block or smash from in front of the attack line.

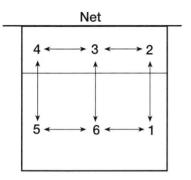

▲ *Fig. 3 Player positions*
▼ *Fig. 4 Rotation*

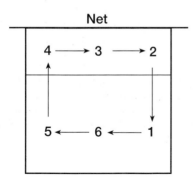

Rotation of players

The same player continues to serve until his or her team loses a rally. When the receiving team wins a rally it wins the right to serve and its players rotate one position clockwise, i.e. the player in position 2 rotates to position 1 to serve; the player in position 1 rotates to position 6 etc. (*see* fig. 4. Note that numbers 1 to 6 refer to the court positions (as in fig. 3) and not to the numbers which appear on the players' shirts).

Before the beginning of each set, the starting players and rotation order of a team may be changed, on condition that the change is noted on the score sheet.

Back row players

The rules prevent back row players from doing two things:

- they may not play the ball directly from within the attack area into the opponent's court unless the ball is below the height of the net
- they may not block.

A back row player can smash the ball, providing the *take-off* for the smash is clearly behind the attack line. The back row smasher can *land* in the attack area.

The game in action

Three touches

Player in position 1 starts play with a service. The team receiving the service is allowed a maximum of three contacts to return the ball to the serving team's side of the net. No more than three contacts are allowed. (A block does not count as one of a team's three contacts.)

Players are not allowed to contact the ball twice in succession (except if one of the contacts is a block).

The normal sequence of play is as follows. Following a serve or an attack, the receiving team attempts to direct the serve or attack towards the net. A specialised player, the 'setter', is positioned at the net, and he sets the ball high and close to the net for an attack player, the 'smasher', to jump and hit the ball down into the opponents' court.

The serving team attempts to 'block' the attack at the net, or to 'dig'

the ball, usually in the back court. A successful block sends the ball back into the receiving team's court and they have another three contacts to set up a counterattack. If the serving team digs the ball they have two contacts, a 'set' and a 'smash', to try to win the rally.

The rally continues until the ball lands 'in' or 'out' of court, one of the teams fails to get the ball over the net within its three permitted contacts, or one team commits a fault, e.g. a player hits the net, or mishandles the ball.

Handling the ball

The rules relating to ball handling, especially on a team's first contact, were relaxed during the late 1990s. This has allowed players to use the volley to receive service, and to play defence without being penalised by the referee for handling faults.

The handling rules are:

- the ball may be played with any part of the body
- the ball must be hit, not caught and/or thrown
- the ball may touch various parts of the body, provided that the contacts take place *simultaneously*.

There are two exceptions:

i) at the team's first hit (when receiving the serve or first attacking) the ball may contact various parts of the body consecutively, provided that the contacts occur *during one action*, i.e. a double touch is allowed.

ii) when blocking, consecutive contacts may be made by one or more blockers, provided that the contacts occur *during one action*.

Simultaneous contacts and double faults

If two opponents simultaneously touch the ball above the net, the player from the team on whose side the ball does not fall is deemed to have touched it last. The other team then has three touches of the ball.

If, after a simultaneous touch, the ball falls on to the court, the team on whose side the ball falls loses the rally. If the ball falls outside the court, the team on the other side of the net loses the rally.

If two players on the same team play the ball and touch it at the same time, it counts as two touches (except in the case of a block).

If faults are committed by opponents at exactly the same time, a 'double fault' is called and the rally is replayed.

Ball 'in' and 'out'

The ball is 'in' when it touches the line of the court.

It is 'out' when: the part of the ball which contacts the floor is completely outside the boundary lines, the ball hits an object outside the court, e.g. the ceiling, or the ball touches the posts, antennae, or net outside the sidebands.

The service

The service is the act of putting the ball into play by the right back row player (*see* fig. 3, player in position 1). The ball must be tossed in the air or released before being served. The server is not allowed to strike a ball resting on the other hand. The ball must be hit with one hand or part of the arm.

At the moment of service the server must be standing in the service zone behind the baseline. If using a jump serve, the server must take off from behind the baseline. It is a fault if the server touches the baseline before striking the ball.

After the service the player may step on to or land in the court.

The server is not allowed a second attempt, even if the ball is allowed to bounce on the floor after the initial toss.

The service is considered good if the ball passes:

• over the net into the opponents' court, and
• between the two vertical antennae marking the width of the net.

The service is a fault if the ball:

• passes over or outside the antennae above the net
• touches a player or object (other than the net) before going into the opponents' court
• goes under the net
• falls outside the limits of the court.

If the serve is faulty, the referee indicates 'side out', and the opponents win a point and gain service.

A served ball which touches the net and passes over to the opposite side remains in play.

Net play

If the ball touches the net during play and passes into the opponents' court, it is not a fault. Even if the ball goes into the net, it can then still be played by any player other than the last one to touch it, providing that the maximum of three touches is not exceeded. If the force of the ball hitting the net causes the net to come into contact with an opposing player, this does not constitute a fault on the part of the latter (*see* below).

It is a fault if a player touches the net when playing the ball. If two players from opposing teams simultaneously touch the net, this is known as a 'double fault', and the point is replayed.

It is not a fault for a player to touch the posts.

Playing the ball above the net

When blocking, a player may play the ball when it is still on the other side of the net, provided that he does not interfere with the opponents' play before or during the latter's attack hit. It is a fault to play the ball on the other side of the net before the opponents have finished their attack.

A player is allowed to pass his hands beyond the net after an attack hit, provided that the ball contact was made on his side of the net. It is a fault for the player to reach over the net to attack the ball or to touch the net on the follow-through from the smashing action.

Contact under the net

Players are permitted to touch the opponents' court with a foot (feet) or hand (hands), provided that some part of the foot or hand remains in contact with, or directly above, the centre line.

It is a fault if any other part of the body contacts the opponents' court.

Substitutions

Each team is allowed a maximum of six substitutions per set. A player who starts a set and is then substituted may re-enter the game, but only for the player he originally replaced. Neither the starting player nor substitute can be substituted again in that set.

Only the team captain or coach can request substitutions and only when the ball is dead.

If a team becomes incomplete through injury to any player and if all other substitutions have been used, a substitute can replace the injured player even if he has already played in another position. This is an 'exceptional substitution'.

'Libero' player

The libero is a specialised defensive player who can only play as a back-row player. The libero enhances the defence aspects of the game and is selected for strong back court defence skills and service receive skills. The libero is often used to replace taller, less agile players in back court. He *is not* allowed to serve, complete an attack hit (ball above the height of the net) from anywhere on court, or to block. Another player may not complete an attack hit if the ball has been volleyed by a libero in the front zone. The libero is, however, allowed to set up an attack from behind the attack line.

The libero can be substituted for a player in the back row, provided that the ball is dead and the whistle for service has not been blown. The libero wears a shirt of a different colour from his team-mates. Each team is free to use a libero or not.

Time-outs

Each team is allowed to call two 'time-outs' in each set to receive advice from their coach. The players leave the court and go to the free zone near their team bench. Each time-out lasts 30 seconds.

Fundamentals

There are a number of basic psycho-motor (mental and movement) skills which underpin all the individual and team skills in volleyball. They are known as the 'fundamentals' and they recur sequentially during play.

The 'fundamentals cycle' is shown in figure 5. The four key stages are:

(1) ready for action
(2) right time, right place
(3) ball control
(4) link and finish.

It is easiest to understand what each of these stages means by describing what a player does during a particular action, for example, when he is receiving a serve.

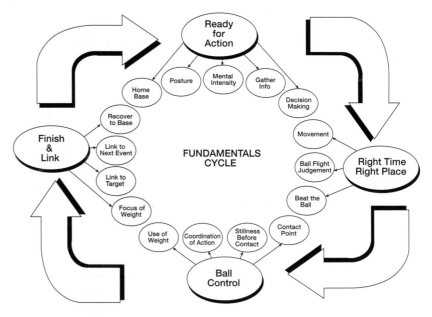

▲ *Fig. 5 (See pages 19-21)*
The fundamentals cycle

(1) Ready for action

- Base position – where do I stand on court in order to be in the best position to cover all of the area that is my responsibility; where do I stand in relation to my team-mates?
- Posture – am I ready physically to move quickly to get to the ball: feet shoulder width apart, knees slightly bent, balanced?
- Mental intensity – am I focused and concentrating?
- Gather information – what type of serve is the server going to use, in which direction is the server likely to serve?
- Decision-making – where is the ball going, do I play it or do I leave it, do I use a volley or a forearm pass to receive the ball?

(2) Right time, right place

- Ball-flight judgement – accurately read the flight of the ball, and anticipate the position to which I have to move so that I can play the ball with control.
- Movement – move to play the ball using the correct footwork, or move to support the receiving player, or move to prepare to attack. Keep hips and eyes level as you move.
- Beat the ball – time my movement so that I get to the contact position before the ball is ready for contact.

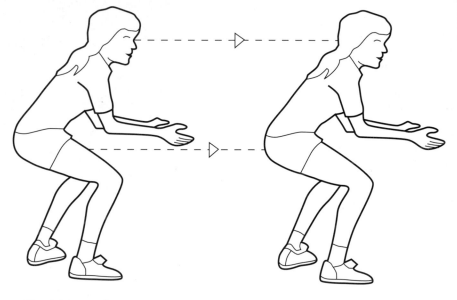

▲ *Fig. 6 Move ready*

(3) Ball control

- Contact point – I have to be behind the ball, to contact it between my waist and knees with my arms about 45 degrees to the floor.
- Stillness before contact – be balanced before contact; mentally focus on the target to which I want to pass the ball.
- Co-ordination of action – use my legs, hips and arms in the right sequence.
- Use of weight – control the speed and trajectory of the ball by transferring my whole body-weight in the direction of the target; don't swing my arms.

(4) Link and finish

- Focus of weight – I need to focus all my weight where my arms contact the ball.
- Link to target – I must finish my action/movement in the direction I want the ball to go (follow-through); I must see the ball going to the target in my mind's eye.
- Link to next event – having passed the ball to the setter, I must move to attack or I must move to cover the smasher.
- Recover to base – the ball has gone over the net; I must move to my defensive base position in order to get ready to defend against the opponent's attack.

Skills

Service

The serve is used to start every rally. It is the only move in volleyball in which the player has complete control. Every player should develop a serve that is low risk so he can be certain of getting the ball into court, e.g. an underarm serve. Players should also work on a serve that can be used to put pressure on the opposition - a ball that is accurately placed or is travelling quickly. There are three main serves used, which are described here.

Underarm serve

- The left toe points at the target (for right handers).
- Weight is on the back foot.
- Perform a simple throw. The arm moves in a straight line. Weight moves forward.
- Arm and body weight move towards target.

Overarm serve

- Stand with feet shoulder-width apart, the left foot facing the target and the right foot behind and to the side of the left foot. The knees are slightly flexed.

- Hold the ball out in front with the left hand at shoulder height.
- Toss the ball with the left hand and at the same time draw the hitting hand and arm back with the elbow high.

▲ *Fig. 7 Underarm serve*

22

- Transfer the weight from the right foot to the left foot and propel the hand through to contact the ball with the palm of the hand.

Jump serve

The jump serve is an advanced serve used by players to generate speed and power (*see* photograph, right).

- The ball is tossed high and in front using the left, right or both hands.
- The player approaches the ball as if preparing to smash the ball at the net, i.e. left, right, left foot pattern (*see* fig. 11).
- The player must take-off from behind the baseline but is allowed to and inside the court after ball contact.
- The ball is contacted high and in front of the body.

▲ *Fig. 8 Overarm serve*

Forearm pass

The forearm pass, sometimes called the 'dig', is used to play a ball that is travelling too fast and low to volley. It is used most often to receive the serve or an attacking shot from the opponents.

The player should move behind the ball and, when it is in front of them, play it between waist and ankle height, and between the legs. The forearms are brought together to form a platform from which the ball rebounds.

- Assume a 'ready to play' stance.
- Move ready in line with the ball flight.
- 'Bump' the ball – don't hit it. Follow to target.

▲ *Fig. 9 Forearm pass*

Volley pass and set

The volley is a two-handed pass that is played when the ball is above the forehead. Once mastered it is the most accurate method of passing the ball.

The volley is most commonly used to set up an attack. The ball is played high above, and about 1 m back from, the net so that an attacker can jump and smash it down on to the opponents' court. This is called 'setting' the ball, and the player who sets is called the 'setter'.

The setter is a key person in the team, controlling and directing the attack rather like the quarterback in American football. He has the option of setting the ball 'high', 'medium' or 'quick' to attackers approaching from the front or behind. Teams usually play with one or two specialist setters.

The volley is also used to receive a slow-moving ball from the opposition (called a 'free ball') and pass it to the setter at the net.

Sometimes a team is forced to volley the ball over the net on the third touch. If this happens the ball should be played as low and as flat as possible into a space between two players, thus making it more difficult for the opposition to control the ball.

- Assume a 'ready to play' stance.
- Watch the ball.

- Be ready to play the ball: on the mid-body line; above the hairline. Bend the knees and face the firection in whic you wish to play the ball.
- Touch the ball.
- Move body weight through in the direction of the ball.

▲ *Fig. 10 Volley pass*

25

Smash

The 'smash', called the 'spike' in the USA, is the main attack shot used in volleyball. The smasher runs in and jumps with both feet close to the net (about 1 m away), striking the ball with one hand down into the opponents' court. Variations that the smasher may use include:

• smashing a high set diagonally across court or down the line
• smashing a quick set – the attacker jumps at the same time as the setter sets the ball
• hitting the ball off the block and out of court
• hitting a controlled, slower smash (off-speed smash) accurately into a space
• or tipping the ball just over the top of the block into the space behind it (similar to a drop-shot in tennis).

At a higher level of play, teams normally have two or three smashers approaching the net from different positions and at different times (e.g.

one for a quick set in position 3, one for a high set in position 4 (*see* figs 3 and 4)). The setter decides which player is best to set the ball to. These multiple attack options make it more difficult for the defending team to position its block and defence.

• Swing the arms back.
• Jump off two feet.
• Lead with the non-hitting hand.
• Control the landing on two feet with no forward travel.

▲ *Fig. 11 The smash*

26

Block

The block is the first line of defence against the smash. It may be performed by one, two or three front row players who jump and reach across the net with their hands to deflect the smashed ball back into the opponents' court. The block can also stop the smasher from targeting a particular area of the court, thus channelling the ball to where the back court defenders have been placed.

A two-person block is most common in volleyball because it the best compromise between strong blocking and adequate court defence. It is too easy to smash past a single blocker, and if a triple block is used there is too much court for only three defenders to cover.

- Stand about half a metre from the net, elbows forward, hands in front of shoulders, knees slightly bent.
- Side step into position.
- Jump and stretch.
- Reach up and over the net. Spread your fingers.

▲   *Fig. 12 The block*

Floor defence

If the ball is hit past the block the defenders must try to keep the ball off the floor and if possible pass the ball to the setter (so that a counter-attack can be set up). If the defender has anticipated correctly and moved to the spot where the ball has been hit, he will then be able to stay on his feet and use either an underhand dig or an overhand defence shot. On many occasions however, the player will have to use a sprawl or dive to get to the ball.

Game cycle

A volleyball rally follows a cyclical pattern of play. It is not enough to know how to execute the fundamentals and skills of the game. Players must be able to move from one phase of the game to the next and know how to recognise the cues (gather information) which help them to make the right decisions about what to do next.

When one team is in a particular phase of the game, their opponents are in the corresponding opposite phase as shown in figure 13.

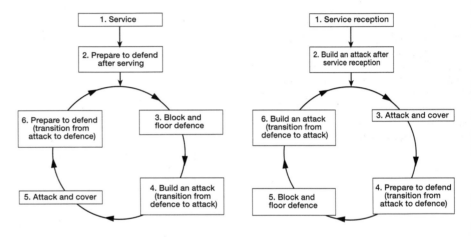

▲ *Fig. 13 Cyclical pattern of play in a volleyball rally*

Team tactics

The sequence of diagrams in figures 14–21 describe how a team might organise itself as it moves through the sequential phases of a typical volleyball rally. A key feature of successful teams is their ability to move smoothly from one phase to the next, e.g. from attack and cover (*see* fig. 18) to defensive positions (*see* fig. 19), to block and floor defence (*see* fig. 20).

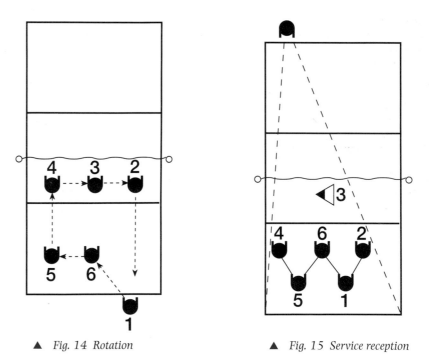

▲ *Fig. 14 Rotation*

▲ *Fig. 15 Service reception*

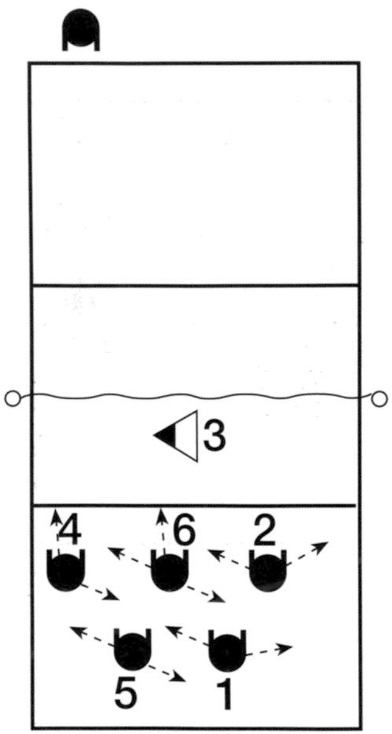

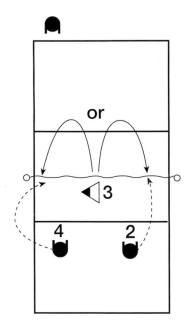

▲ *Fig. 16 Movement in service reception*

▲ *Fig. 17 Setting up an attack*

or

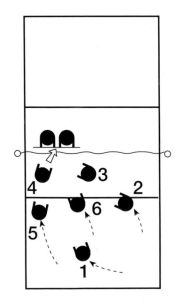

▲ *Fig. 18 Attack cover*

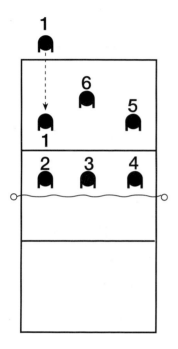

▲ *Fig. 19 Defensive base*

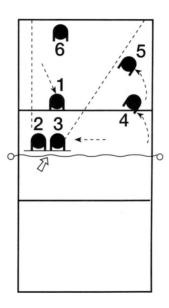
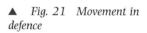

▲ *Fig. 20 Block and floor defence*

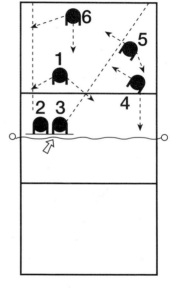

▲ *Fig. 21 Movement in defence*

Officials and sanctions

In official competitions a first referee, second referee, scorer and four line judges are required. For some matches a team of six ball retrievers are used to operate a three-ball system, minimising delays between rallies by ensuring a ball is always ready for the server at each end. At a lower level one referee and a scorer is often adequate. Figure 22 shows the typical positions of the match officials.

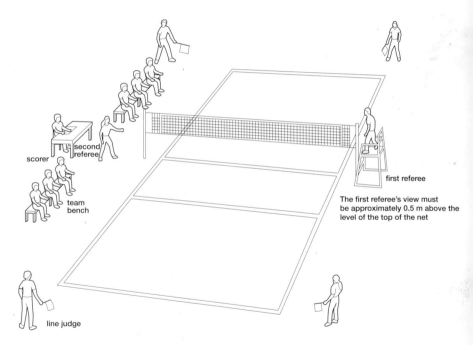

scorer

second referee

team bench

first referee

The first referee's view must be approximately 0.5 m above the level of the top of the net

line judge

▲ *Fig. 22 Positions of match officials*

The first referee

The first referee is in overall control of the match and his decisions are final. The first referee is positioned on a stand above one end of the net. The referee whistles for service, and to signal the end of each rally, indicating the fault or action which ended the rally and which team has the next service.

The first referee is responsible for calling serving faults, and judging ball handling and faults at the top of the net. The first referee is also responsible for disciplining any inappropriate behaviour and may act on the advice of the other officials.

Sanctions

There is a four-tier scale of sanctions in volleyball:

(1) a 'verbal warning' is given for a first, minor offence, e.g. time wasting or showing dissent. There is no penalty to the player or team

(2) a 'yellow card' follows a second minor offence or a first more serious offence, e.g. rudeness to the referee. The player's team loses the rally (a point is given to the opposition)

(3) a 'red card' is awarded for any offensive conduct towards the officials or opponents and the player is sent off for the remainder of the set. If a player is sent off, a *legal* substitution may be used (*see* page 15, 'Substitutions'). If no legal substitution is available then the team is incomplete (only 5 players) and it loses the set

(4) any aggressive conduct or threat of aggression is punished immediately with 'red and yellow cards jointly' and the player is sent off for the remainder of the match.

The second referee

The second referee stands on the floor, off the court, opposite the first referee and is responsible for checking the rotational order of each team, calling faults at the bottom of the net and centre line, and controlling time-outs

and substitutions. The second referee must also check for a back row player blocking or attacking from inside the attack line.

The scorer

The scorer sits at a table behind the second referee and completes the scoresheet by recording team lists, the rotational order of each team in each set, points scored, time-outs, substitutions and any cards given by the first referee.

The line judges

Two or four line judges can be used and they make decisions on 'ball in' and 'ball out'. They also indicate to the first referee if the server has committed a foot fault, if the ball touches the block before landing out of court ,and if the ball crosses the net outside the antennae. Each line judge has a flag.

Hand signals

The officials do not usually speak to the players; they communicate their decisions using a whistle and hand signals. Only the team captain is allowed to speak to the referee and then only to ask for an explanation of the decision given. The most common signals used by the first and second referee and line judges are shown in figure 23.

team to serve next

ball 'in'

time-out

change court

misconduct

ball held

end of set

delay in service

▲ *Fig. 23 Hand signals*

four contacts

positional fault

ball 'out'

double contact

reaching beyond the net

net touched by a player

service authorisation

crossing the centre line (or ball underneath net)

blocking fault or screening

double fault

team delay

ball touched

substitution

back-court attack-hit

37

Scoring

The team winning a rally scores a point and the right to serve.

In the first four sets the set is won by the first team to reach 25 points, with a two-point advantage, e.g. 25–23, 26–24, 35–33. The fifth, tie-break, set is played to 15 points, but again a two-point advantage is needed to win, e.g. 15–13, 16–14, 22–20.

Official matches are played to the best of five sets for both men and women. Some competitions, especially those for young players, are to the best of three sets, and in local tournaments matches often have a time limit, e.g. best of three sets, each set a maximum of 15 minutes.

The International Rulebook and Official Scoresheet are available from the English Volleyball Association (*see* address on page 1).

Duties of participants

Players

Players must know and abide by the rules. They must accept the referees' decisions without disputing them. During the game only the team captain can speak to the officials.

Coaches

The team coach can either sit on the team bench nearest to the scorer's table or stand or walk within the free zone in front of the bench. The coach can give instructions to the players during the match.

The coach can call time-outs and substitutions.

If a team does not have a coach, the team captain assumes all duties.

Beach volleyball

Beach volleyball is played on the same size court and with the same net heights as volleyball (18 m x 9 m; 2.43 m men, 2.24 m women). International competitions are played with teams of two players (no substitutes are allowed).

Scoring and matches

In beach volleyball only the serving team can win a point. If the receiving team wins the rally it gains the serve but does not win a point. Rally point scoring may be introduced in the future to bring beach volleyball in line with the indoor game.

Matches are one set only to 15 points. If the score reaches 14–14 play is continued until a two-point lead is gained (16–14, 17–15). However, there is a 17-point limit so if the score reaches 16–16 then 17–16 wins the match.

Differences between volleyball and beach volleyball

• There are no centre line or attack lines on the court.
• Players can go 'under the net' provided they do not interfere with the opponents.
• The block counts as one of a team's three hits.
• If a player volleys the ball over the net it must be played in a direction at right angles to the player's shoulders.

• Teams switch ends after every five points.
• Teams are allowed four time-outs each.
• No coaching is allowed during the match.
• The ball is softer – 0.175 to 0.225 kg/cm2 on the beach; 0.3 to 0.325 kg/cm2 indoors.

41

Park volleyball

The International Volleyball Federation has introduced a new form of recreational volleyball 'park volley' which is normally played outside but can be played indoors as well. It is played 4 v 4 and the teams may be single sex or mixed. The court is 14 m x 7 m and the net is 2.43 m high for men, 2.3 m for mixed and 2.24 m for women. Rally point scoring is used, each set is played to 25 points with a two-point advantage required to win the set, and matches can be one, two or three sets as agreed by the teams.

Sitting volleyball

The main differences in sitting volley-ball are:

- the court is 10 m x 6 m and the net 1.15 m (men) or 1.05 m (women)
- some part of a player's body from the buttocks to the shoulders must remain in contact with the floor
- the serve can be blocked
- a player's position on court is judged by the buttocks, so it is permissible for the feet or legs to touch the baseline on service, or to go over the centre line etc.

Only players with physical disabilities can play in international sitting volleyball matches. Club-level sitting volleyball is played by integrated teams of disabled and able-bodied athletes.

Starting out

Volleyball is a simple game which does not require any expensive equipment. It is suitable for all ages from eight-year-olds up to 'young-at-heart' pensioners. When starting to play, or when first introducing the game, do not play six-a-side immediately; instead play small-sided games, e. g. 3 v 3 or 4 v 4 on a smaller court so that everyone gets more opportunity to play the ball and learn the skills more quickly.

The table opposite summarises the English Volleyball Association recommended progression for introducing and developing volleyball with young people.

Adapted rules

- Up to and including 4 v 4 the ball may only be contacted on or above the knee.
- A 'fast-catch' volley is allowed in under 10 (U10), under 11 (U11) and at local beginner-level under 12 (U12) competition.

References in table

(a) Court dimensions are the regulation size and should be used when courts are being specially marked. As many sports halls have badminton and netball lines, the following dimensions can be used.
(b) Use badminton court inner lines: 11.88 m x 5.18 m.
(c) Use badminton court inner back lines and outer sidelines: 11.88 m x 6.1 m.
(d) Use badminton court outer back lines and outer sidelines: 13.44 m x 6.1 m.
(e) An alternative for inexperienced players playing at local level is to play 'Short Court 6' on a 16 m x 9 m court. This can be achieved by putting a net along the long axis of a netball court (30.5 m x 15.25 m) to give up to three volleyball courts 15.25 m long x 9 m wide. One sideline on each court needs to be marked.
* Girls may play in a boys team up to and including U14 age group competition.

AGE	GAME FORMAT	COMPETITIONS	COURT DIMENSIONS[a]	NET HEIGHT BOYS	NET HEIGHT GIRLS
U10 and U11	2 v 2	Mixed	6 m x 4.5 m	2.15 m	2.15 m
U12	3 v 3 (mini volleyball)	Mixed	12 m x 5 m[b]	2.15 m	2.15 m
U13	3 v 3	Boys* or girls or mixed	12 m x 6 m[c]	2.15 m	2.15 m
U14	4 v 4 (Volley 4)	Boys* or girls or mixed	14 m x 7 m[d]	2.15 m	2.15 m
U15	6 v 6	Boys or girls	18 m x 9 m (16 m x 9 m)[e]	2.24 m	2.15 m
U16	6 v 6	Boys or girls	18 m x 9 m	2.35 m	2.24 m
U17 and U18	6 v 6	Boys or girls	18 m x 9 m	2.43 m	2.24 m

Teaching guidelines

Here are some guidelines to help make the teaching of the game fun and successful.

- Use light-weight teaching volleyballs or foam balls - neither of these will hurt beginners' hands. Do not use soccer balls, netballs or moulded rubber balls.
- If a volleyball net is not available, use a rope with coloured braids attached as court dividers.
- Position the net lengthways down the centre of the gym or sports hall. This provides space for a number of smaller courts rather than only one large court. Many small-sided games give more ball contacts and playing opportunity than one six-sided game.

- The net or rope should be higher than the reach height of the tallest child. This ensures that attack shots have to be high thus giving the defenders more time to react to the ball. This helps rallies become longer, which is more fun.
- Introduce competitive games right from the start. Allowing weaker players to catch and throw the ball in 1 v 1 and 2 v 2 games, while they are gradually learning the volley skills, means everyone can have fun right from the start.
- Emphasise the use of basic tactics from the beginning, e.g. attack from near the net; move back early to defend your court; attack to an empty space.

- Rules should be introduced gradually and when appropriate. Don't be too strict, especially on handling, at the outset.
- Make up special rules to help achieve the learning aims, e.g. there must be at least two touches before a team can return the ball over the net.
- In the early stages, don't stop games too often to correct errors. Instead, work with individuals to improve their personal skills.
- Provide practices and drills at which the beginner can be successful.
- It is essential that every player should learn the fundamentals of each position (setter, smasher, etc.), so that they appreciate the demands of each role. Don't let players specialise too early.

Index

48